BLESSINGS

FOR THE

HOME

Honoring God's Presence
in *Every* Room

DANIEL CONNORS

TWENTY-THIRD PUBLICATIONS
twentythirdpublications.com

TWENTY-THIRD PUBLICATIONS
One Montauk Avenue, Suite 200
New London, CT 06320
(860) 437-3012 or (800) 321-0411
www.twentythirdpublications.com

Cover photo: © iStockphoto.com / Maya23K

ISBN: 978-1-62785-443-6
Library of Congress Control Number: 2018962306
Printed in the U.S.A.

A division of Bayard, Inc.

CONTENTS

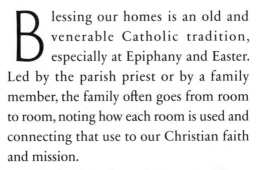

B lessing our homes is an old and venerable Catholic tradition, especially at Epiphany and Easter. Led by the parish priest or by a family member, the family often goes from room to room, noting how each room is used and connecting that use to our Christian faith and mission.

Let's borrow from that great old tradition and spiritually walk through our houses, even without leaving our most comfortable chair. We can do this anytime. Let's stop in each room to consider how faith is alive in these spaces, to increase our awareness of how God is working in ordinary things, and to pray for God's abundant blessings.

Before we start, however, there are two important things to remember:

First, the heart of our faith is a reality the Church calls the *paschal mystery*—how Jesus, out of love, gave up his life for us all, and by rising brought life to the world. We speak this reality at every Mass when we proclaim the "Mystery of Faith."

But this Mystery of Faith is not just about what Jesus did—it's also about us and what we do "through him, with him, and in him." Jesus invites us to be part of this paschal mystery by joining our lives to his dying and rising and living his life in our own.

We became part of this paschal mystery in our baptism, and it grows in us as we participate in Eucharist and in all the sacraments. And one of the startling truths of our faith is that, as we grow in the paschal mystery, we actually share more and more in the divine life of God, and we have an opportunity to bring this divine life to the world in all the events of our ordinary, often mundane, daily lives.

Little by little, through all the experiences of our lives, good and bad, joyful, sorrowful, and in-between, we learn to "die" to our own self-centeredness and unhealthy, selfish desires and, instead, to practice compassion and forgiveness and generosity—to grow in love for others. Dying in Christ in this and many other ways, we live in hope of rising with him to new life. Dying and rising—this is what being a disciple is all about.

In this book, we'll mention the paschal mystery from time to time. This is because, ideally, home is one of the most important places where we learn to be disciples and live this paschal mystery more deeply. It's one of the places where we learn to make room for others, to find balance between our needs and the needs of others, to grow in love in many ways, to have our unhealthy egos cut down a notch or two, and to find the courage and support and learn the wisdom we need to go beyond the home and reach out to others. It is also one of the places where flashes of the sacred, of resurrection and transfiguration, can pop up and dazzle us at any time. The home is a holy place of "dying and rising," a school for disciples.

Second, remember that we all experience "home" in different ways throughout our lives. At the moment, you may be part of a family with children. You may be a couple. You may be living alone. No matter. As you read and pray with this book, think of all the ways you have experienced "home" during your life. Some of the memories may be happy. Some may be less so. But all these experiences, good and bad, are part of home for you, part of your life, part of your path of discipleship, and they are worth praying over and blessing God for.

And remember too that some of us live in huge houses, some in small studio apartments. But while these differences often matter a great deal to us, Jesus tells us they matter not a bit to God. So please feel free to adapt what we offer here to your own situation.

With that said, let's begin where we usually do with a home—with the front door.

The
FRONT DOOR

S top and take a long look at your front door, and your back and side doors if you have them. Look beyond any scratch marks or peeling paint or any smudges on the door glass.

Consider instead how solid the door is, what it sounds like when the wind and rain and sleet beat against it and how the door (and the house as a whole) shelters you. At bedtime do you double-check to make sure the doors are locked? I do. These doors are our family's defense against the dangers of the night.

Now think of God, who does the same. "I come to you for shelter," the psalmist cries (25:20). "Protect me, keep me safe, and don't disappoint me!"

But our doors are more than barriers; they're entry and exit points, portals between our private, domestic world and the rest of life. We pass through them to go to work, to the store, to school. We kiss our spouses and children goodbye there. We practice hospitality at our doors, greeting friends and visitors and occasionally a person in need, and we practice patience and courtesy as we deal with a variety of salespersons and religious evangelizers. The front door can be the paschal mystery in action—no matter how much we might want to be alone, somebody knocks. The world calls us out of ourselves.

Let the door slam shut, and think of how we too are a door, a portal—for it is through us that Jesus enters into and interacts with our world. We can open wide to let him come through us to others, or we can slam shut inside ourselves and keep God's grace from breaking through. How widely do we welcome the world? What opportunity to grow in holiness is about to ring the doorbell?

PRAYER

Lord Jesus, you said "Behold, I stand
at the door and knock."
Help us to be aware of all the ways
you come to our door.
Help us to see you in our neighbors, friends,
and strangers who come knocking.
May our door open wide
to the needs of the world,
but slam tight against prejudice, violence,
and anything that hides you
from our sight.
Be our shelter in times of trouble,
and may all who pass through this door
know your saving love. Amen.

The
LIVING ROOM

L iving room...Is there such a thing anymore? In the old days, houses were supposed to have front parlors reserved only for entertaining guests. Houses today have great rooms, combination living and dining rooms, family rooms, rumpus rooms, TV rooms, and fully equipped kitchens with giant flat-screen TVs connected to the internet, and easy chairs. Whatever we call it, you get the idea: This space is where we do our "living"—everything from entertaining guests to sprawling on the sofa with a tablet or a ball game. And whatever we call it, it's the center for a whole lot of faith connections.

Think about this living space, no matter where in your home it is:

- Sit in the chairs and on the sofa and think of the people you've welcomed in this room over the years. Look around the room and see what they saw—what this room tells them about you every time they come here. The hospitality you offer, the warmth you show: What are these but reflections of the warmth and hospitality God shows us—our God who sends messengers out to invite all to the wedding feast? Every time we offer warm welcome and hospitality, we show the face of God to the world.

- Think of the times you came home from work too tired for anything but just sitting in this room. Sit on the sofa and think of the times you sank into its cradling arms for a nap, or to check Facebook, or cuddled up on it with a spouse or child or pet. Think of our Lord, who said, "Come to me, all you who are weary, and I will give you rest." Praise God for the comfort and rest you've found in this room over the years.

- See the floor covered with Legos that jam up your vacuum cleaner and stab your bare feet. Think of all the stuff strewn all over the coffee table or floor. Watch or remember the children squealing and running through the room. Think of family members all sitting here but each absorbed in their own phone or tablet. Think of the patience this room has helped you practice, all the fights and squabbles that started or ended here. All of this, too, is a course in holiness, in dying and rising with our Lord.

Think of the holiday seasons and birthdays celebrated in this room. The decorations, the singing, the Christmas tree, the warmth of family and friends, the squeal of delighted children. Think of opening presents and trying to gather up yards of ripped off wrapping paper. And never forget that each gift given in love is a way of sharing in the life of God, who is the greatest gift-giver of all.

• Look about and think of how much this living room has helped shape who you are. If you are new to this house, think of the promise this room contains: like our Christian life, bursting with possibilities.

Look around and remember too the people who sat or played or talked in this room or rooms much like it, but now no longer do. The family and friends that life and death, each in their own ways, have taken from you. Perhaps your parents, or a brother or sister, or your spouse, or even a child. Remember happy moments with them in this room, and sad moments too. And if tears come to your eyes, let them fall; the deep ache of loss never really goes away. Take the sadness you feel in losing them and lift it to God, so that God may share your grief, comfort you anew, remind you that they are still with you in love, and nourish your hope that you will all be together again in God's kingdom of risen life and love.

Thank God for it all, the good and the bad, the joy and, yes, even the sadness this room represents. And remember that God's promise is for abundant life. Praise God for all the living and all the hope that this room holds.

PRAYER

Jesus, you came so that we might have life,
*   and have it to the full.*
I thank you for all the living
*   that goes on in this room.*
Help me to remember that when I show
*   hospitality*
I am living in you,
*   for you welcomed all who came to you.*
Help me find rest in this place, and love.
Help me to see your grace alive
*   and active here,*
whether the room is full of family noise
*   and chaos, or whether I sit here alone.*
Put your arm around me
and breathe rest, comfort, joy,
*   and life into my soul.*
And remind me to thank you,
*   all the days of my life.*

The
BEDROOM

Walk into your bedroom now, and take a look around. Look past whether the bed is made or not, or the dog or cat is sleeping on it or not, or the closet is bursting with clothes or shoes, or the dresser is covered in spare change and knickknacks. For now, just think about your life in this room.

Think of the bed first—the place where most of us start and end our days.

- Here is the place where we have one last opportunity to bring the events of the day to God, to thank God for the day's joys, to ask for help with its sufferings and anxieties, and to express sorrow for the times, that day, when we missed opportunities to live the life God calls us to. In the morning it gives us our first opportunity to thank God for another day of life and to focus on how we will live our faith in action that day. Morning and evening prayer can be as simple as turning our thoughts to God for a brief moment.

- Here is where some of us sleep soundly but others toss and turn, our minds restless with the events of the day or tomorrow, or anxiety about finances or children or jobs or relationships. "Day and night I went without sleep, trying to understand what goes on in the world," laments the sage of the Book of

Ecclesiastes. And what could be worse than thinking you're wide awake when even God is sleeping? "Wake up!" cries the psalmist. "Do something, Lord! Why are you sleeping?"

I used to think just asking God to let me fall asleep would work. It didn't. Often around three in the morning I begged and pleaded. Gradually I realized a poor night's sleep, and the frustrated, honest cry of the psalmist, are both parts of the paschal mystery. God usually does not save us from life's trials, big or small. Perhaps in the long run such trials can teach us to look beyond ourselves. To stop thinking the world is here to meet our needs or work on our schedule. To learn patience and compassion for the weaknesses of others. We don't have to go out looking for trials: life provides plenty of opportunities. But God also wants us to be honest, even if it means yelling out in anger and frustration, "Wake up, God! Do something!" There is nothing so bad, or so ordinary, that we cannot bring it to God.

- The bed is a veritable reservoir of opportunities for growing in holiness. Here we express and grow in love with our spouse. Here begin the children who, all by themselves, are compact little universities of our education in the paschal mystery: through them we learn to love and live for others instead of just for ourselves.

- Sit on the bed and think of the times it's given you comfort and rest and an opportunity for great joy, when it's nestled you in illness, when children came running to it because of things going thump in the night, when you spread outfits over it trying to decide what to wear for that special occasion. Think of the dreams you had in it, and remember that the prophets Samuel and Daniel, and Joseph and many others, all heard God speaking to them in dreams. Look over at your closet, full of the clothes that help you express who you are, and perhaps whom you wish to be, the outfits that, like faith itself, are meant to bring you joy.

An ordinary bedroom is an extraordinary place. So many aspects of life and love intersect here. It can prepare us for the world outside, or we can roll over and go back to sleep and miss bringing our gifts to God's world. It can remind us of all we have to celebrate in our lives. It can challenge us to think about how we spend our time and money, and whether we're leading the life God wants us to share.

Look around your bedroom. What does it say about you? How do you find God here? What signs of God's presence might you be missing? What will you bring to God this evening as you get into bed?

PRAYER

Jesus, you said the birds have nests
and the foxes their dens,
but the Son of Man has no place
to lay his head.
Let me thank you first that I have a place
when so many people in our world do not.
Help me always to be compassionate
and generous to others.
Let my last thoughts at night be with you
and my first thoughts in the morning too,
and in the middle of the night when sleep
has fled, thank you for being there,
wide awake with me,
so that I may share with you my deepest fears
and frustrations, and my greatest hopes.
May I hear you call to me in this room,

and may I leave it wide awake
   with your strength,
ready to do your will, to meet you and be you,
   among all the places and faces I encounter.
And when I return here, tired and frazzled,
may this room be a place of
   rest, comfort, love, and strength,
   all the days of my life. Amen.

The KITCHEN

There's no doubt about it. This is command central. Even if you store dishes in your oven, think the Iron Chef is the Tin Woodman's cousin, and believe the best recipe you've ever heard is "1) pick up your phone, 2) order pizza," the kitchen is still the center of the world. Let's face it: a room that has both a refrigerator and a cookie drawer is a holy place, a place worthy of pilgrimage day or night.

Think of the relationships that are built in this room. We might lament that everyone is so rushed in the morning or so scattered in the afternoon and evening, but why not be grateful for the gravitational pull of this room, and the natural opportunities it gives us to encounter one another? Think of good friends sitting at the kitchen table, building their friendships with you over a cup of coffee or tea, the quick family conversations on the way out to the car, the children sitting and doing their homework while having a snack. A little ice cream providing an excuse for a late-night chat between mother and daughter. The kitchen is a natural relationship builder. And few things are more Catholic, or holier, than building loving relationships.

And the food! How often Jesus speaks of the kingdom of heaven as a banquet, a wonderful feast! Jesus' enemies called him a glutton and a drunkard, and he does seem to have enjoyed a good meal. Remember the time he called to Zacchaeus in the tree and said, "Zacchaeus, come down. I am spending today at your house"? I can easily see Jesus walking in to the kitchen and checking what's simmering on the stove.

Food is full of holiness. After life itself, food was God's first gift to Adam and Eve. God fed the Hebrews in the desert—not just manna but quail. Jesus multiplied bread and fish to feed thousands. And Jesus comes to us in an extraordinary way in every Eucharist under the forms of ordinary food and drink.

Even the busiest of families gather at least occasionally around the table for special meals together. Eating a meal together is one of the oldest and richest of human customs—a sign of deep hospitality and love. Shopping and preparing food for your family, and sitting and eating and sharing food with them: all this is holy work—a sign and precursor of the sacrificial meal we share at Mass at the table of the Lord.

At various times when you are in your kitchen:

- Stop for a moment and look around. Take in these familiar things and how you've shaped this room over the years, and how it has shaped you. What are your most cherished memories here? Bring each up in your mind and heart and thank God for everything this room means.

- Breathe deeply and take in the wonderful smells of food cooking, coffee brewing, even water boiling. Remember how this room smells when Thanksgiving dinner is being prepared, or the scent of any special meal you've had here. Hold these smells and aromas all in your heart and think of them as previews of the heavenly banquet Jesus promises.

- Listen to the sounds of life all around you: the kettle whistling, eggs sizzling, lettuce crackling, milk or juice slurping out of the carton. Listen to the voices of family members laughing or arguing or complaining. The little squabbles and teasing at the breakfast table. The sounds of loved ones hurrying off to the day. The sound of a friend sharing her heart with you. The singing of Happy Birthday, and the whoosh of breath as candles are blown out.

  Listen to the quiet when you are alone here. Listen to life. Cherish it all and give thanks to God.

- Pick up ingredients and mix them together. Open a loaf of bread. Think about how these ordinary things connect you to the wide world of humanity and nature. The farms where the produce is grown, the field workers who harvest it, the shippers who send it toward you, the supermarket employees who stock the shelves—you are never eating alone. Think about your own place in this large human chain. Give thanks to God.

- Touch the back of the kitchen chairs. See your loved ones sitting there. Touch the counter you've wiped clean a million times. Thank God for such a place to prepare the simple meals and the great feasts. Think of the love that has been expressed in this room in so many ways. And praise God for the joy of being alive!

PRAYER

God, at Mass the priest blesses you
for the bread
"fruit of the earth and work of human hands."
In the same way I thank you
for the grace of my kitchen,
where ordinary things also become
extraordinary gifts of love,
where human hands I don't even know
have joined with me to feed my family.
Help me to cherish all the
wonderful expressions of love
in my kitchen,
and let me never forget the poor
and the lonely and the hungry.
May all who pass through my kitchen
feel the warmth and welcome of your love!

The
BATHROOM

I f ever there was a room in our house
to humble us and remind us that we
indeed have bodies and are not angels,
it's got to be the bathroom.

It's hard to hold a spiritually exalted
opinion of oneself while taking care of the
most basic of bodily functions. And it's
hard (thankfully not impossible) to hide
from the reality revealed first thing in the
morning in the bathroom mirror—the face

unmade-up or unshaven, the hair askew, the eyes heavy with sleep, those extra pounds that sneaked up on us, or just the effects of time's passage. This is a moment, and a vision, to be shared only with God.

It may not be pleasant, but at the very least it's an important reality check. It's a reminder that God always sees the truth of us. We cannot hide physically, emotionally, or spiritually from God, and it's always best not to try. We should never be embarrassed about being totally honest with God.

What we may find hard to imagine is that God sees us as we see ourselves in the bathroom—and still finds us fully lovable. Why else would God have chosen to be born among us, to live among us in Jesus, who shared these same embarrassing bodily functions and may not himself have looked or smelled his best early in the morning or after two or three weeks walking the hot and dusty roads of Palestine—

not to mention forty days in the wilderness.

Since the time of Jesus there have been various Christian groups who felt the body was evil and sinful, something to be pushed away so that the soul could be free. The Church, though sometimes affected to some extent by these groups and their way of thinking, has always held on to the belief that the body is God's good creation, something sacred to be honored in life and in death. We believe, says the Creed, in the resurrection of the body: in the fully realized kingdom of God, we're not going to be disembodied souls.

The human body is so important that St. Paul uses it to help explain how our entire Christian community is the body of Christ. "God put our bodies together in such a way that even the parts that seem the least important are valuable," St. Paul says. "He did this to make all parts of the body work together smoothly, with each part caring about the others. If one part of our body hurts, we hurt all over. If one part of our body is honored, the whole body will be happy. Together you are the body of Christ. Each one of you is part of his body." Think of that the next time you catch a look at yourself in the bathroom mirror.

So many of our sacramental actions involve the body. The water poured over us in baptism; the oil lavished on parts of our bodies in baptism, confirmation, ordination, and anointing of the sick; the bread and wine transformed into the Body and Blood of the Lord. We wash; we rub; we eat. Water, oil, bread, wine—all common physical things full of unfathomable grace.

So the next time you are in the shower, enjoy the feel of the hot water washing over you. Enjoy, even revel, in the sensation of the water on your skin, cleansing, refreshing, soothing. Let it speak to you of the cleansing, soothing, life-giving qualities of baptism. If you anoint yourself with oils and fragrances, let them be signs of the fragrance of heaven, the life of the Spirit, of God living and active in our midst.

At some moment of every day, make it a point to stop and enjoy the sensations and wonder of physical life. Listen to the sounds of birds in the trees, the quiet of falling snow, a bumblebee around your flowers. Feel the warmth of the sun on your face, the wind in your hair, the kiss of your lover, the cat purring on your lap, the baby in your arms. Take a long look at something in your home you just never seem to notice. Marvel at the wonder of small, insignificant things.

Go into the bathroom and remember how sacred you are—body and soul—and how loved by God.

PRAYER

Jesus,
by being born into our world as one of us,
you confirmed God's judgment in Genesis
   that creation and human life are both
   very good.
Thank you for making me body and soul,
so that I may enjoy the delights
   of your creation,
   the loving touch of another,
and all the joyous and sometimes
   scary and painful sensations of being alive.
Help me see and cherish
how my body connects me to your world
   and to all of humanity,
   and how I am part of your body.
Help me to accept it all as your wondrous gift.
Help me to reverence your creation,
and to reverence myself, as you do. Amen.

The
CHILDREN'S
BEDROOMS

Whether your child's bedroom is in the crib stage, the stuffed-animals-everywhere stage, the "Keep Out! This Means You!" stage, or the empty-nest stage, here is another part of many homes bursting with grace.

Let's think of it this way: Police academies have mock street setups to teach recruits proper police procedures. Fire academies have practice houses that they burn down regularly to teach recruits how to fight a fire. In a similar way, having and rearing children teaches parents a great deal about living the paschal mystery.

How? Consider the famous Last Judgment scene from Matthew's gospel: Jesus says, "When the Son of Man comes in his glory with all of his angels, he will sit on his royal throne…, and he will…say to those on his right, '…Come and receive the kingdom that was prepared for you before the world was created. When I was hungry, you gave me something to eat, and when I was thirsty, you gave me something to drink. When I was a stranger, you welcomed me, and when I was naked, you gave me clothes to wear. When I was sick, you took care of me, and when I was in jail, you visited me.'"

Having children is a great way to practice and grow into this kind of discipleship.

Our children are hungry, and we feed them.

They are thirsty, and we give them something to drink.

They can be a stranger—from not fitting into a clique at school, to feeling like they are strangers to themselves, and at times strangers to their parents—and we do our best to welcome them and let them know we care.

We clothe them.

We nurse them when they are sick.

And while some of us actually do have to visit our children in prison, all of us visit our children in the various mental, emotional, and physical prisons they build for themselves or have thrust upon them, and we do what we can to move toward forgiveness, reconciliation, and healing.

In each of these ways, parents learn to give of themselves for others, to put the needs of others before their own—dying to self and rising to new life! It's all paschal mystery living. It is simple, ordinary holiness in action.

Of course, it's just a start. Jesus wants us to take the holiness we practice in our families and extend it to everyone. Jesus loved children, but he seems to have had a fairly unsentimental view of families, especially families that keep all that discipleship bottled up inside the family. It isn't enough to consider yourself a member of a specific family and to share with them and them alone. "My mother and my brothers," he said, "are those people who hear and obey God's message." Jesus challenges us to widen our definition of family. What we learn in here needs to move out there.

- Stop by your child's room. Think of your memories. Hear the songs you sang to them when they were little. Remember the "new baby" smells. Hear the laughter and giggling, and the whimpering cries of "Mommy" or "Daddy" in the night. Remember the stubborn battles over bedtime or vegetables. Remember holding your sick child and wishing you were the one with the fever instead. Praise God for all these times.

- Think too of the stomping and the door slamming, the times when things weren't going so well and forgiveness needed to be asked for or given. Think of the childhood phases you prayed would end soon, and the ages at which you wished your child could always stay. Think too of your own childhood relationships with your parents—the good and the bad and how they shaped you. Lift it all up in prayer and thanksgiving (and if some memories are very bad, think and pray about how you might move toward healing, and who might help you on that difficult journey).

- Touch something cherished by your child (do this carefully if you have a teenager!) and remember where and how they got it, and what it tells you about them.

- Think of the person you were before your child was born. Think of how he or she or they have changed your life, slowly transforming you into the person you are and are becoming. Could you even have imagined where life is taking you, the good and the bad?

That's what entering into the paschal mystery does for us. That's why we need to enter deeper and deeper into it in every Sunday Mass. Slowly over a lifetime we die to the old self and rise to new life in Jesus. Slowly over our lifetime, Eucharist and paschal mystery living shape us into the persons we are, and are becoming.

Look at your child's room, and give thanks for it all.

PRAYER

*Jesus, I know I have not always been
an A student when it comes to
    parent and child relationships,
and often I have no idea
    where this school of discipleship
    is taking me.
I trust that you know the way.
I trust that you will be with me
    in all the joys and sorrows I encounter.
Teach me, please, to see
    the signs of holiness you plant everywhere.
Help me to learn patience, forgiveness,
    and generosity in all that I do.
Help me to realize that your love for me,
    and everyone, is even stronger than
    the love I have for my children.
Help me be a sign of your love to them,
    and to everyone I meet.
Be with us all, as we grow and learn. Amen.*

The
CHRISTMAS
TREE

Not a room, but a focus of most homes for a season or more, and deserving of some thought.

On a Christmas eve, almost sixty years ago, a family I know was sitting on the floor by their Christmas tree, the children in their pajamas, their faces lit only by the lights on the tree. For the past half hour or so, they'd been singing Christmas carols—"Away in a Manger," "Silent Night," "O Little Town of Bethlehem," "Joy to the World"—all the classics.

Then one of the older children noticed that his little brother wasn't singing. He was just sitting there, looking at everyone. Having just turned three, he didn't know any Christmas carols yet, so he really wasn't able to take part. Immediately everyone started talking about what song they could sing that the little boy would know too.

Then they realized the perfect song—and suddenly their voices joined together in a rousing rendition of the Mr. Clean® commercial jingle. The little boy's face lit up with recognition, and he stood and bounced joyfully up and down as he joined in singing about cleaning the "whole house and everything that's in it."

When it was over, everybody cheered and hugged. Christmas was here, for everyone.

That little boy's older brother has never forgotten that night. In the light of a Christmas tree, and out of love for their youngest member, a family turned a TV jingle into a Christmas carol. Love transformed something secular into something sacred— and made a family moment very holy.

Christmas trees are like that too. Some complain that it's a secular custom, basically serving as a place to put the mountains of presents that our consumer culture tells us to buy more and more of. Some complain that we put trees up way before Advent even begins, or that we keep them up way after the Christmas season ends.

There is some truth to all of this. But Christmas trees with all their bright lights are also signs of joy and hope in our hemisphere's darkest time of the year. In a world so aching for hope and joy, can you blame people for putting them up early or taking them down late?

Think of your Christmas tree, and your trees of Christmases past. It doesn't matter if they are small and on a tabletop, or huge and filling a front window. When you and your family and friends gather around it, it becomes something holy, a sign of God giving hope and joy and Jesus to the world, a sign of your love and care for one another.

Think of the gifts given and received around your tree—gifts ideally chosen and given in love and in the hope of being received with joy. And remember that giving in love is what God does all the time. It's what God did for us in Jesus. And it's what Jesus asks us to do in our family, and in the world.

We never get it exactly right; we never do it perfectly, not the way God does. But every year we put the tree up again as a sign to the world, and to ourselves, that hope is alive. We practice gift-giving, ideally hoping to learn in it something about giving more of ourselves out of love. And if we look closely, we might catch a glimpse of the truth that the presents around our tree, and the songs sung and toasts made and hugs shared near its branches, all proclaim that Jesus is here, and Jesus is love.

PRAYER

Jesus,
St. Luke tells us that
    when you were born,
your parents placed you in a manger,
    a feedbox for animals.
Luke seems to be telling us that,
    even then, you were the Lamb of God,
    food for a hungry world.

Jesus, our world is so hungry today,
hungry for peace, hungry for hope,
    and in many places, hungry for food itself.
Bless our Christmas tree

and all who gather by it.
Let it be a sign to us of the hope
you bring to the world.
Let it remind us of the holiness
of this season and all of life.
May the hope and joy we experience
here by our tree
inspire us to find ways
to bring joy and hope to others,
and to join you in being food
for a very hungry world.

OTHER PARTS
of the HOME

How important it is to take a moment now and then to remember the blessedness of life and the abundance of grace around us! Grace is here, even in times of sorrow and sadness. Here are some examples from other parts of the home we've not yet explored:

- Look at the spaces your pets call their own and think of these creatures who share your home and have become part of the family, giving you more opportunities to give and receive love (and sometimes practice patience!). The dog who is so happy to see you, no matter when you come in, and so often comes to you with a ball in its mouth and that "let's play" look in its eyes. The regal cat who makes such a show of ignoring you as it jumps up on the windowsill to sit in the sun but will sometimes allow you to stroke it while it sits in your lap and purrs. Bird, dog, cat, gerbil, iguana, and on and on. We feed and care for our pets, and they feed our souls. It is an exchange of holy love. Thank God for them!

- Look at the TV area and think of the times you and your family have watched shows together and laughed and cried together. What gifts these are to cherish! Think of how the TV and the internet connect you to the wider world and help you share in our culture—the good and the not so good, the uplifting and noble, and the rude and crude. What an opportunity the TV, the internet, and social media give to practice moral choices, to decide where our values lie, to question aspects of our culture and our roles in them!

- Next time you are in the garage or the attic or the basement or are opening a closet door, stop for a moment and ponder what all these areas say about you. What do we store? What can't we part with? What half-finished projects are looking back at you? What kind of choices have we made over our lifetime about what is important to us? What's parked in the garage? Our hearts, says Jesus, will always be where our treasure is (Matthew 6:21).

- Garages and basements often contain our tools. Before there was Bob the Builder there was God the builder. God is building a world, and a kingdom, and God invites us all to join the work. Building, constructing, and repairing what is broken can all be powerful images of Christian discipleship. And helping build a world of justice and peace, and working to protect Earth as a home for humans and all creatures, is more important today than ever. Praise God for whatever tools and skills you have, and ask God to help you use them to serve the wider world.

- The yard and the deck. Our buffer zone to the outside world. A place of rest and refreshment, but a seductive temptation to stay put and or let the rest of the world go by. What does our use of these spaces say about the choices we make?

- The apartment balcony. A wonderful place to look out at the world and to gather with friends, a vantage point to reflect on the world and our place in it. What do you see from your balcony? Whether the view is humble or grand, bring it to God in your prayer.

- The computer, tablet, smart phone, internet, social media—more connections to the wide world, and so important to us all that they deserve being mentioned again. They all present an opportunity to learn, play, and be part of humanity, when used well. And when used poorly they can lead to isolation and even hatred of others and oneself. Making choices is always part of the human and the Christian adventure. May God always help us choose wisely.

Praise Our Generous God!

When it comes to income level, number of possessions, and comfortable living, most of us are doing OK. We're not rich, but we're not poor either. Even so, budgets can get stretched tight, and many of us can spend ourselves into trouble in a hurry.

How different God is from us! God

is the last of the big-time spenders! God never hoards resources, never budgets, never asks the price, never gets frightened at the thought of spending lavishly, never runs out:

Life? Here you are!

Forgiveness? Always yours for the asking, in whatever quantity you need!

Grace? Sown like seeds on any kind of ground there is.

Salvation? Take it; it's free!

God never stops spending. And the signs of it are all around us, as we hope our little house blessing tour has shown.

This is only the beginning. But we can get so caught up in living, being so busy about so many things, that the signs of grace God plants everywhere can escape our notice.

Whatever the object, whatever the space, go on a treasure hunt in your own home. Look for the extraordinary in the ordinary, the faith connections that too often pass us by. Watch and listen for the signs of love, life, forgiveness, the hard work of reconciliation going on day by day, the choices that bring us closer to God or push us farther away. From the moments of greatest joy to deepest grief, listen for the all-too-easily missed sound of God at work.

On Sunday at Mass, we enter into the paschal mystery. Every day, let's bring that faith home.

And thank God for it always!

PRAYER

Jesus,
in John's gospel you say,
"Make your home in me
as I make mine in you."
How wonderful it is, Lord,
to realize that you are
making your home with me,
that you are here with me in my home
and all the events of my life.
I don't have to worry
about making room for you,
for you are already here with me, always.

Blessed are you for the home you and I share.

Blessed are you for all who have shared this
*   home with me, both now*
and in the past
and in the years to come.

Blessed are you for all I have learned
—and am learning here—
about living with you, in you,
and through you.

Open my eyes and ears, Jesus,
to all the holy signs and sounds of home.

Open my eyes so that I may see
you in my ordinary home,
and my ordinary life.

Open my eyes to all the dazzling,
startling sparks of holiness and divinity
that surround me,
if only you help me look for them.

In the same way, Jesus,
open my ears!
Remove the earbuds of
self-importance that
keep me focused on myself,